OTHER BOOKS BY ROBERT M. DRAKE

Spaceship (2012)

The Great Artist (2012)

Science (2013)

Beautiful Chaos (2014)

Beautiful Chaos 2 (2014)

Black Butterfly (2015)

A Brilliant Madness (2015)

Beautiful and Damned (2016)

Broken Flowers (2016)

Gravity: A Novel (2017)

Star Theory (2017)

Chaos Theory (2017)

Light Theory (2017)

Moon Theory (2017)

Dead Pop Art (2017)

Chasing The Gloom: A Novel (2017)

Moon Matrix (2018)

Seeds of Wrath (2018)

Dawn of Mayhem (2018)

The King is Dead (2018)

For Excerpts and Updates please follow:

Instagram.com/rmdrk
Facebook.com/rmdrk
Twitter.com/rmdrk

ISBN: *978-1-7326900-0-4*

Book Cover: Robert M. Drake
Cover Image licensed by Shutter Stock Inc.

Sometimes the most beautiful people are beautifully broken.

For The Lovers.

CONTENTS

DAWN OF MAYHEM

ROBERT M. DRAKE

MACHINES

People don't need to be fixed.

They are not machines.

They are not
devices we can turn off
or on
whenever we'd like to.

Whenever

we feel the need
to be entertained.

People are so much more,
and what they really need is

attention,
time
and kindness.

They need love
and not just any kind,

but they need the kind
that doesn't slip away.

They need

someone to listen to them,
to understand them.

Someone to hold them
when they feel alone.

When they feel
as if they don't have enough
to carry on.

So there it is.

People are people
and they're not broken.

They're not empty
and they're definitely not lost.

Everyone is right
where they need
to be,

and there isn't a damn thing
we could do
to change that.

Our lives mean so much more
and we must find the light
within ourselves
to set one another free.

THE QUESTION

Is it too much to do?

To chase your dreams
and *follow your fucking heart?*

To clear your head
and do all the things
that make you happy?

Life is about perspective.

About how you allow
certain places,
events
and people affect you.

It's about
collecting memories,
not things.

About
living in the moment,
not dwelling in the past
or the future.

And above all,

life is about finding soul

in all places
you never thought
you would.

Life,
above all,
is about

holding on to
the people you love

and letting go
of things
that bring you harm.

TRUTH IN ME

I have no desire
to fit in.

No plans
to walk with the crowd.

I have my own mind,
heart
and soul.

I am me

and it

has taken me years
to realize
how important that is.

BLOOD IS BLOOD

I carry the dreams of my ancestors,
the bones of their past

and the legacy their children's
children
have long forgotten.

I carry hope,
the pain of many generations,
before me.

Both of blood
and tears

and within its depths
I seek truth.

The truth of self.

The truth of freedom
and equality.

Who am I?

I ask beaten,
exhausted and tired.

Alone in cold dark rooms,

the chambers of my mind…
the hallways of my heart.

I am *not* empty.

I am *not* broken.

I am not what the mind controllers,
the crooked leaders,

the shameless
unlawful manipulators
want me to be.

I am strong
and through my journey
I will find the boiling sun.

And it will burn in my hand
but it will not cause me harm.

It will not bolster nightmares
and dead stars.

It will not expand to horrors
but lessons and growth
and gifts from the gods
themselves.

This is now…

If there is a space within me,
it is full of movement

and it is full of space dust
and the chaos of life.

The chaos of wanting more
of wanting to become new.

I am more.

I am blessed.

I have a sack full of air
in my lungs.

And I couldn't ask for more.

Not today
or tomorrow
because the future
belongs to me.

My life belongs to me.
My thoughts.
My feelings.
My fears
and my joys.

They all belong to me.

I am here.

I am now.

I am right where I need to be,
and I am carrying

both the known

and

the unknown

through the strengths
of my past

and through the pain
of everything

I have ever felt.

RETRACTION

You can't change people
but you can change yourself.

And if we all decide
to do so,
to change

this world can become
a beautiful place.

Because kindness is a blessing,
understanding is a lifestyle

and hate can still be
one of those things
we hear about,

but never had
the opportunity
to feel

for ourselves.

DO WHAT YOU MUST, HEX

My cousin Hex
and I
are driving to the beach.

A long drive
about forty minutes

from start to end.

The sky is bright.
The sun is out.
The air is as cool
as it can be.

He turns over
and mentions he has to
use the restroom:

He has to pee.

Five minutes pass.
Then ten.
Then thirty.

We are at the tip
of our destination.

The waves,

the liquor
and the sand await
in their glory.

It's not going anywhere.

He can't hold it anymore. .

Desperate
and in pain.

The urge to let go arrives.

Pulsating.
Pulsating.
Pulsating.

He tells me to pull over.

I cannot pull over.

"We are in the middle
of traffic," I say.

Stepping on the gas,
and then stepping on the brake,
and then clutch.

I shift gears.

He finds an empty bottle

from the other night.

Without shame he unzips
and releases.

The flow of things.
Things that flow.

He sighs like the *mother fucker*
that he is and laughs.

He gets what he wants
because he needs to
because he must.

Because there is no other way
to go about it.

And it goes...

because nothing stops
because you want it to.

Everything keeps going
and going
and going...

no matter how badly
you need it to halt,
to stand still.

You have to do
what you have to do...

and sometimes,
when you have to,

you have to pee in a bottle.

You have to suck it up
and just do

with what you have.

YOU CAN NEVER

Isn't it sad

how sometimes
you can never tell

the difference
between pain
and love.

Between lost opportunity
and possibility.

Between what people say
and what they do.

Between being loved
or being used.

Perhaps
that's why

I sometimes feel
like I don't belong.

Like my head
is somewhere else
and my heart

is floating
beyond me,

somewhere

in the clouds.

CANNOT WRITE

I want to write you
a goddamn poem
but I don't have the words
to say what's in
my mind,
my heart.

Because it's not *that* simple.

What I feel,
what I want

is as

complicated
as it gets.

Because that's how it is.
It's never fair.

When people want something,
they always go about
the wrong way to get it.

And when people don't
want something
that's when it presents itself,
you know?

And it's sad
how this happens.

How you chase
but never receive.

How you receive
but don't know what to do with it
when it is finally yours.

And it's the same
with love and people
and places and things

and almost everything
you can possibly begin to imagine.

We never get what we want,
when we want it

and when we do,
it is either too late

or we don't know
what to do with it

at all.

BEHIND THE SHADOW

What we leave behind
becomes the past

and sometimes

the past
doesn't define us.

It's a misrepresentation
of how we see
ourselves.

A DARK DAY

I met a girl with a bird tattoo.

I asked her
what it meant to her,
why she would ink her skin
with it.

She said it meant freedom.
That some time,
in her past life
she felt caged.

She felt imprisoned
by her own life,
her own choices.

She said she wasn't living
for herself.

That she was married
and forced into it
by her parents,
by almost everyone she knew.

She said
her life was full of darkness.

Full of chaos

and madness
and emptiness.

She was lost
and now she is found.

And I asked, *"why the bird?*
why does it represent
that part of your life?"

And she looked me in the eyes
and carefully said,

"Because I'm a bird, baby,
and it took me six years
to find my wings.

I am free and there is no limit
to what I can do."

Since then,
I've thought about what she said
in hopes that maybe one day—I, too,
would find my own pair of wings.

That one day—I, too, would feel free.

And that one day—I, too,
would find the courage to believe.

Until then,

this is my life:
Dreaming of what it's like to fly.

Dreaming of what it feels like
to taste the sky.

The world is beautiful
but *nothing is more beautiful*
than feeling free.

Amen.

DO NOT BECOME GLASS

I do not want
to see you fall apart

because all things
that are soft—break.

And all things
that break

should never be left
unattended to fall.

Therefore,
I will hold you
and carry you

no matter how tired
my arms are,

and you will blossom
like no other.

You will light
the fucking sky

and there's nothing
anyone

can do
to stop that.

I guarantee it.

THE ORIGINAL

Have a little
control over yourself.

They want you
to fall.

They want you
not to fight
and accept their laws
and revolution.

They want you
to abide
and not ask
any questions.

They want you.

And that is the keyword.

These companies
that are killing the world.

That are destroying
the family.

The original man
and woman.

The original God
and religion.

The original
school of thought
and feeling.

Yes.

These companies.
These products.

They need *you*
 more than you
need them.

And they don't want
you to know
the truth.

I am no genius
but it is as clear as day
to know this.

And it should be clear
as day
to live by this.

The foods cause cancer.
The vaccines cause autism

or other defects.
The media is brainwashing
the children.

And Hollywood is full of shit.

In long black streets
and in lost forgotten avenues,

we have all
lost our way.

Our eyes.
Our minds.

And our hearts...
as televised.

There is war
and war is always at dawn,

and it is
brighter than ever.

We are all under attack.
Our children

and elderly are deep within
the zones of battle.

No longer can we think.

No longer can we be ourselves.

Read, I urge you to.

There is something stirring
from afar

and it is far worse
than terror.

Far worse than bombs
and buildings falling.

Imagine this...

living in a world
where our identities
no longer exist.

In a world
where we can no longer be
who we aspire to be.

*There is a war
going on outside that
no one is safe from.*

And the glass shatters
and the people scream
and the dogs howl

and none of us
can think for ourselves.

THE OCEAN PEOPLE

The sea knows
more about me

than I know
about myself.

The ripples share my story
and I am not broken.

I am not worthless
or weak or easy
to manipulate.

I am the wave that devours.

The force of both
destruction and creation.

And yes,
I am a little hard on the edges.

A little lost
and a little confused

about how I feel
but nonetheless,

I do not give

a flying *fuck*
about other people's opinions
of me.

I take my time
and I accept myself
for what I am…

regardless

of how it makes
other people feel.

TELL ME

Tell me exactly
how you feel.

Tell me why
you've distanced yourself

and why the space
is comforting.

Tell me what I can do
to make you feel
at home

and what I can do
to give you
what you need to heal.

Tell me about your wounds,
the scars you're hiding.

The ones too sad
to ignore.

Tell me about the people
you've given too much to

and the ones
who've left you behind:

Empty
and even more
confused.

Tell me about
what's keeping you awake
at night.

About your horrors
and worries.

Tell me.

You can trust me
with all of your flaws.

Tell me,
and I will show you

how you are worthy
of love and belonging.

Tell me
because isn't it time
someone did things for you
for once?

Isn't it time
someone put you first?

You don't deserve this pain,

this terrible search
for something
that's not even real.

You deserve so much more,
and you deserve the space
within you
to be filled with love.

To be filled
with a kindness
so deserving

that only the ones
with a broken heart
understand.

Because you've earned it.

Make today
the kind of day

that starts
and ends with you.

SPEND OUR LIVES

Isn't it sad
how most of us
spend our lives

planning for a future
that isn't secured.

How we fly
through the present

and don't appreciate
the moments
that bring us happiness—until

it's too late.

And how we convince ourselves
we'll have another chance

to relive

everything

we choose to ignore.

BOOK SIGNING

I had a special book reading
one night in Wynwood.

It was one of those moments…
I barely do these

but my sister convinced me
to do so.

She says

it'll be a good look for me.
A good way to give back.

There were 500 people,
by invitation.

It lasted longer
than expected
but it's okay.

It's for the readers
and *I'll do almost anything*
for the readers.

A random girl comes up to me,
after signing over two hundred books.

She takes a picture and says:

"One day,
I want to be like you.
I want to be
a bestseller
and I want to be
in the charts.
I want to do it
on my own.
Like you."

I took a sip off
my vodka on ice.

I inhaled, looked her in the eyes,
and opened myself to her.

I said,

"My dear,
these charts
and bestseller lists
are meaningless.

It's just another way of control.
Another way the system
keeps everything on check.

Another way
to devalue ourselves

and place us between
the fangs of war
and jealousy and envy.

My dear, these lists,
they don't make you
a great writer,
an influential writer.

Which ultimately
is
what most writers want
to be.

What to leave behind.

My dear,
these charts are fixed.

Publishers pay *these lists*
to get their books on there—
to make the population
buy their books—
to reach the masses.

It's all an illusion.
A mockery of the art.
A mockery of the people…

and what they feel.

These lists.
These charts.

If you want to be
like me,

I continued.

*"Then stay away
from this system."*

Because once they have you,
it is impossible to break free.

And the publisher
will make it hell.

They will try to ruin you
before you can find
your freedom.

This, most writers…*must learn.*

To be for the people
then there is no need

for the corporation
to milk off you
off your art, off your heart.

This, most writers…*must learn.*

To move people,
is a process
and it is something that takes
a lifetime

not something that can be bought
overnight.

This, most writers…*must learn.*

To be successful
you must do it for yourself
before anyone else.

You must do it because
you must
because it is the only
thing you know how
to do.

This, most writers…*must learn.*

Once you do it for yourself
soon enough
all the success will come.

She didn't say a word after that.

She just smiled
and nodded.

And I never saw her again.

A few months later
that same girl became
a *New York Times* bestseller.

And she never thanked me
for what I said.

The light will always
defeat the darkness
and the light

will never ask
for anything

in return.

SOME THINGS YOU DESERVE

There will be
some things
you won't get over.

Some things
that will sting so hard
they will set you back to
where you started.

And you will hurt
and hurt and hurt.

But you will also
rise from it.

You will learn
from the past.

And you will adapt
and survive

no matter how hard it gets.

You will shape
your own reality and accept

how you should never
settle

for anything less
than you deserve.

This should be *gospel*
for all who walk the Earth.

For all who dream
and for all

who know
they can be

so much more.

THE BUS STOP

Waiting for the bus
one afternoon during college.

The day was flaring.

My eyes barely opened
because of the heat.

I waited with the same
intensity of someone with nothing
to lose.

An Indian girl approached the bench.

She had on a gray sweater
with red stripes running
from arm to arm.

Her hair fiery, wild,
out of control
but somewhat in control
like branches stretching from
a burnt down tree.

There was this look about her.
She looked like an artist, I thought.

My eyes were drawn to her.

My soul was captured

and the next moment
she sat by me and began
to look around her bag.

She pulled out her cell phone.

Began to text
or search for something.

She laughed.

Then looked around
before putting her phone
back where it came from.

I looked away,
and then back
and then away again...

I am doomed.

I felt something coming
from the core of my stomach.

A slow sting,
one that I am attracted to.

From afar the bus
was finally in view.

From a distance.
I got up
and picked up my belongings.

I swung by her
as I awaited
the arrival of the bus.

She looked at me

and

I looked at her.

I smiled

and then

she smiled.

"Excuse me," I said.

She nodded as she tucked her legs
and looked down

as the bus
made a complete stop.

I boarded the entrance
and looked back at her.

She returned the favor
and smiled...

then nodded her head once again.

A light ignited in my eyes—
a fire that only the broken
would understand.

And just like that...

She was gone.

She was lost
and she was never
to be seen again.

Like a ghost.
Like a memory.
Like an idea stirring
within my imagination.

Did I make her up
in my head?

Every now and then
I ask myself this question.

And for the past twelve years...
every once in a while

I think of what
became of her.

That's what it takes.

One day.
One moment.
One person…

to change your life

forever.

And to this day,
I wish I could have

asked for her name
or what interested her.

Anything…

then perhaps,
if so,
my life would be different

whether
I was expecting someone
like her

or not.

AFRAID OF LOVE

You got it all wrong.

You shouldn't be
afraid of love
or people who genuinely care.

You should be afraid
of credit debt,

student loans
and cancer causing foods.

Those kinds of things
haunt you forever,

no matter how far
away you go.

And love,
my dear,
well...

it is our most valuable
possession.

So if I were you,
I'd keep my head up.

I'd learn how
to carry on,
and believe in the color
of love.

It's all we have.

It's all we'll ever need.

Everything else
was built to destroy you.

To put you in a box
without ever
asking for reasons
why.

BEEN HERE TOO MUCH

And still,
there are somethings
about ourselves

we are not meant
to understand.

Some parts
we know exist
but don't know why.

These are the little
intricacies that pull
people like us
together.

To do
the silly little things
we do,

without thinking twice.

To cry,
laugh, and love,

without knowing
where it'll all end.

If this is something
we're not meant
to know,

then let it be ours
for a little while.

Let the feelings we feel
bring us a thousand moons
and let the people

we don't want…
leave, be gone.

Because I want you,
here and now.

And I don't want
to lose this moment
forever.

Let hanging on
to one another

be the best decision
we've made

since

we've been here.

STOP STOP STOP

Stop giving yourself
to people

who don't understand
their own feelings

because some people
don't water
their own hearts,

and expect *you*
to stay

when they *fail*
to care

for yours.

NOT WHAT IT CAN BE

This is not
how it ends.

This is how
it keeps going.

This is the next chapter.

The connection between
two points:

The past and the future.

This is how you learn
to walk again.

To run and fly.

This is how you stop
and realize
how your history was meant
to guide you

but doesn't necessarily
define you.

This is how you learn
to smile again.

This is how you don't
apologize for your mistakes
and take back
what you deserve.

This is how you regain
whatever it is you've lost.

This is how you accept
that your life

is continuous
and it doesn't stop
everytime you crash.

This is here.
This is now.

This is what you should
be doing, feeling, chasing.

This is who you are.
This is who you want
to be—the fallen sign
you've been looking for.

If there is any other day
to be yourself,

this is it.

Today,
of all days,
can be yours.

You can still
hold on to something.

You can still
become yourself,

and reach for the planets
and stars

above your head—like no one
has ever

done before.

THEY SAY...

They say you can't choose
who you fall in love with.

That it is something
that happens
on its own.

And I'm still here.

Searching for you
in every woman I meet.

Searching for myself
in people...in places,

asking God what does it take
to be happy.

If happiness exists
in myself or with her...
another person.

This feeling
of abandonment
welcomes me home.

Welcomes my writing,
giving me something

to cry about.

To bleed over.

You can't choose
who you fall in love with.

I agree.

We all do…

but the reasons to let
love find you
aren't enough.

It sort of happens,
whether it's the wrong
or right person.

It must.

Bottles dry out.
The room becomes colder.

My hands.
My arms swing into the air
to catch nothing.

To catch a space
that you once filled.

What you've built
within me
is far too high
to get over.

I am broken,
lost in a sea of people

and none of them
have the directions
I need to find my way
back to you.

Back home.

They say you can't choose
who you fall in love with.

And that saying
might be true.

But you can choose
who to let go.

Who you leave behind.

And although,
it hurts,

I started living with you
but also dying

at the same time, too.

And now I can't choose
what it is I feel.

I can't control
how I'm going to
spend my day.

If I am going to rise
or drown…

beneath the waves.

And sadly,
I never knew
this kind of pain
could last this long.

The heart keeps beating.
The memories keep fading

and all the sounds
I hear…

remind me

of you.

HURT YOU

Maybe it's hard
to let people know
how you feel.

To show them
how much you care.

To love them
without putting yourself
at risk.

Maybe it's terrifying,
although,

you've tried to convince
yourself you're not afraid.

Not afraid to lose.
Not afraid to burn,

to make sense
of all the things

you can't figure out
on your own.

Maybe it's not too late
to send someone a message.

To tell them
how much you miss them.

How much
you still care

and how bad you feel
for *fucking up*

the way you did.

Or maybe it's not too late
to forgive someone
who's done you wrong.

To give them your smile
and know
how things will be okay

in the long run.

And maybe it's not your fault
or maybe it is

but at this point,
none of that really matters.

What matters is
accepting all of your flaws
for what they are.
Overcoming the self-doubt

you carry
and letting people know
how you feel

before it's too late.

That's what matters,
in the end.

Being true to yourself
and only yourself.

No matter who you hurt
or how bad

the things you let go
hurt you.

THE BEAUTIFUL THINGS

Beautiful things come
with healing.

You stop looking
for someone to blame.

You start accepting
your flaws

for what they are.

And you release everything
that weighs you down.

You learn to love yourself,
and that's

what matters most.

Not how you fell
but how you got up.

Not how badly you broke
but how you put yourself

back together.

And not

how many people
you met

but how many lives
you changed

as time went on.

SAD ISN'T IT

Isn't it just sad,
you know?

Knowing how there will
be some feelings

we'll never be able
to understand.

Some people
who we'll never be able
to forget.

And some things
we'll never be able to fix

no matter how much effort
we put into them.

That's what hurts.

How there will always be
some places, some people
and some things

that'll make us feel
at home

but we would never have
the opportunity
to claim them as our own.

That's the kind of place
we live in.

We spend our time dreaming
about the things

we do not have
that we barely make sense

of the things

we carry
within ourselves.

NO DESTRUCTION

You said you couldn't swim.

That your body was aching
and your mind was exhausted

but here you are.

Keeping your head
above the waves,

fighting for another chance

and making the best—of whatever
is left of your heart.

Because the world
doesn't just need

another good person.

It needs someone who knows
how to make a difference.

Someone who finds
the future

in the destruction
left by the past.

SHE COMES AS SHE GOES

A friend of mine
comes to me
a little distorted.

She comes with enough tears
to fill a river.

She was in a relationship
for the past eight years,

married.

She tells me about her relationship,
how all she did was give.

She cleaned his clothes.
Cooked for him.
Made reservations.

Was always attentive
to his needs.

In return
she got nothing.

No acknowledgment.
Not even a thank you.

The nerve of some people.

And now she says
she is ruined.

She says
she is empty
and full of shame.

Now she feels nothing.
She is numb.

Cold and forgotten.

I told her there was no reason
for her to feel shame.

No reason for her to feel
as if she could have done more.

It was her right
to feel numb, empty—especially

after giving someone
so much

and not receiving
anything in return.

People meet.
People fall in love.

People break one another.

And almost,
always...

when it is over

some people never seem
to heal.

They just continue
to live without knowing

how to move on.

KEEP YOU ALIVE

You have this heart,
and it keeps you alive

regardless

of how you feel.

Regardless
if you're having a good
or bad day.

And it does so
because that's its duty,

that's its responsibility…
to keep you alive.

And then there's you.

And you have to ask
yourself the same question
to figure things out.

What are you
responsible for?

What are you
doing to keep yourself

alive, to keep yourself
happy, afloat?

Regardless if you're having
a good day or a bad day.

You owe it to yourself
in the long run.

You deserve to be
happy and not because
you want to,

but because

you need to—to keep yourself alive.

The human heart
does what it must
to keep going,

and it doesn't stop
for anyone

and neither should you.

Things don't have to be perfect,
they just have to be

enough
to keep you alive.

SOME BAD THINGS

Bad things
are going to happen,
very bad things.

Some nights
you will think

your world
is going to end.

Some nights
you will feel defeated.

Some nights
you will be exhausted,

and you will feel
as if you've had enough.

As if no one
understands what you're
going through

and

as if you're *ultimately* alone.

Bad things are going to happen.

They must.

And when they do,
you won't be the same.

You'll change,

every

single

time,

you'll be someone else.

Until you look back
and realize *YOU ARE*
someone else.

And you won't even recognize
who you once were.

You'll even wonder
how this change happened,
how your life got
to this point.

Good or bad.

You can blame it
on all the pain you've borne.

On all the good-byes
and on the brokenness
you've been granted.

And you will not notice,
not until
you've been through enough.

And then
you will realize,
how terrible it is,

that your growth depends
on the darkness—
one that blooms
from the depths of your soul.

How your most tragic moments
shape your reality

and how everything that hurts
will eventually
make you whole.

How sad it is,
that we must suffer
in order to appreciate
happiness.

That we must walk
through hell

in order to find
paradise.

Because bad things
are going to happen
but the trick is

to breathe and decide
which things are worth
hurting over

because I get it
and believe me,

I DO...

you're not alone.

SOMEONE TO TALK TO

I want someone
to talk to me
and tell me about their

secrets and fears.

Because I am not empty.

I have filled my own space
and all I really want is

to know what it feels like
to give yourself

away—to someone
who cares.

To exchange pieces
of yourself
with tenderness

and soft hands.

Now tell me
about yourself, love.

Are you ready?
Is the door open?

Are the windows shut
and has your soul
been left unfinished?

Tell me,
who's done you wrong?

Where it all became
a burden for you

and why you can't seem
to find any sleep
at night.

Tell me why you spend
most of your time
alone, searching
through your phone,

looking at other people's lives.

You see,
I'm just like you.

I'm constantly searching
for something that probably
isn't even real.

And the truth is,
all I really want
is for someone

to ask me the right questions
and not leave the moment
I reveal a piece of myself.

Someone who lets me in
and someone who isn't afraid
to stay.

I want someone who's willing
to break me down

when I have nothing
left to say.

NO ONE AROUND

You risk so much
for people who care
so little

and never ask why.

This is the kind of person
you've become.

You give
and never ask for anything
in return.

You speak your heart
without the intention
of being heard

and you spread love
because it makes you
feel good—

regardless
of who's around.

ANOTHER DAY ANOTHER COLOR

Love is just another color.

Another projection,
figment, broken down
by the eyes.

And I've seen enough
to believe it
when I see it.

And now,
my dear,
I am seeing you.

Alive and well,
singing and dancing
and tripping over the beats
of my heart.

I can feel you inside of me.

Picking away
at whatever is left
of me.

At all the things
I'm hiding.
If the world is your oyster,

then please,
my love,
by all means
take it.

Take it all
and leave nothing behind.

Take the light
and the darkness.

The shades of madness
and nothingness.

And the swift air
that blows throughout my lungs.

Take this pain,
this blood,
and all
that worries me.

But please,
my dear,
by all means,

do not break what you've
been given.

What you've taken with
or without permission.

Do not leave it for stray.

Do not let it taste
the foulness of abandonment
and do not let it feel

all the little explosions
that come
with solitude.

Do not, my love.

Do not
because I am fragile.

I am easily shaken up.

This you must understand.

If you want me,
then I am yours
but only take me
because it is all you've ever wanted.

And love me.
Love me with the same intensity
of that
to create a star.

With the same warmth
it takes to comfort life.

So love me now.

Love me in all shades,
in all projections
or forever, let me be.

Let my heart be the forest
you get lost in.

And let your tenderness be
the air that sets me free.

Forever.
Forever.
Forever…

Dearest love,

until my mouth
can no longer pronounce words
and my bones
can no longer hold me together,

I love *you.*

I *always* have

and

I *always* will.

WHEN I AM WRONG

I can admit,
I was scared to lose you,

that's why I cared.

I didn't want to live
without you.

I couldn't see myself
going on.

That's why
I was there.

That's why
I put so much into this,
into us.

It wasn't because of anything else
other than that.

I couldn't see myself
with anyone
and I couldn't stand the thought
of you
with someone else either.

It was you

or nothing,
and I wanted
all of you.

In all metaphors,
sorrows and truths.

I wanted you
and I couldn't move on
without you,

that is,

if you were not
by my side.

But I can admit,
I was wrong

and now
like all things that
come too soon...

 it's too late.

DAMN.

SO MANY THINGS

You can be
so many things,
and yet,

you've chosen to be shaped
by sadness,
to be fractured by it.

You've chosen pain,
hurt, suffering
and you have because
it's the easy way out.

Because you think,
you don't deserve to be happy.

Because your past
makes you believe

you don't have much to offer,
at least not enough.

But you're wrong,
and sometimes the past

is a liar—it can make you believe
you don't deserve any better.

It can change you
into a different kind of person,
into someone
who has forgotten

how to love—how to believe
in the goodness
of the human heart.

It's wrong, it all is,
but not you.

You're not all terror.

You're not all sadness
and tragedy.

You're so much more.

So why do you put
yourself through so much
knowing the difference

between what's right
and wrong.

Between what you deserve
and what you don't.

Why do you let
the people who've hurt you

back in?
And why have you let
so much time pass
doing nothing about it?

You can be so many things,
so why can't you find
the reasons to be happy.

You deserve to break apart
in the company of soft hands

and you deserve a kindness
so gentle—it would make

the flowers wish
they fell from your head.

You deserve,
that's the keyword here.

And once you believe,
you shall receive.

All good things come
to those
who believe

in themselves.

THE TRAGEDY

There are some things
you can't let go.

Some people
you can't forget.

That's life.

You hold on,
you let go
and most of the time

you don't get
what you want

nor

what you deserve.

WHAT COUNTS

It's how you
share yourself
with people.

How you speak to them,
teach them.

How you relate
and exchange feelings,
memories.

It's about finding yourself
in their eyes.

That's what's important here.
That's what counts.

DO NOT KNOW WHO I AM

It's okay if you don't
know what to feel,

if you don't know
what you want
and if you can't

figure things out
as you go.

It's okay to not want something
you worked so hard
to get—after realizing
it wasn't what you thought it was.

It's okay to change your mind,
to make mistakes,
to walk away from someone
you once loved—

from something
that once meant the world
to you.

It's okay,
because this is *your* life,
your cause, your body,
your beliefs, your mind,

your heart,
and your feelings.

And you don't need
validation from anyone,

other than yourself...

and I hope
it doesn't take you
a lifetime

to realize that.

YET TO COME

The best moments
in your life
will be the ones

that almost didn't happen,
with someone
you never expected

and in some place
you never knew existed.

Remember that.

HEAL THE WORLD

Don't use whatever you have left
to spread violence and hate.

Don't become
part of the problem.

Choose love.
Choose laughter.
Choose kindness.

We've all been through enough.

We've all stayed silent
for far too long.

It's never too late to change.

It's never too late to accept
one another for who we are.

All we really want
is acceptance,

acknowledgment and respect.

The world has stripped us
of these things
but we can still get them back.

There's still time,
and there's still
enough love

to heal the world.

IS MONEY ALL EVIL?

For reasons not known,
money is *not* all evil.

Money has some truth
in it, some perspective.

You see,
when you are broke,

(and believe me,
I have been broke
all my life...)

all you think
about is money.

How you're going to make it.

How you're going to pay
your rent, pay for food, etc.

Money. Money. Money.

It becomes your life...
the hustle, the chase.

The struggle.

It becomes everything.

It blinds you

but

when you get a little money
and when you collect

some more and then, even more.

It gives you a sense
of what really matters.

It makes you realize
how *not everything*
is about money...

having money opens the doors
to what really makes you happy.

To what really matters,
oddly enough.

Money...
it helps you realize

what you want to
spend your time on

because

it is no longer
your main priority.

Now it is hard to swallow,
I know

but it is the truth,
the dead truth,

the truth
most of us don't want to see.

Life, family, friends and breath
become a whole lot brighter

once your pockets feel tighter.

Money...

it can do some things
to your life:

not all good
but not all bad either.

And for me,
it has given me sight
to what really matters.

It's all about perspective

and money is not,
hardly if ever,

the destroyer

of all worlds.

THIS CUTS

Isn't it sad
how sometimes

you have to be cold
to get someone's attention.

How sometimes
you have to do
what's wrong to make sense
of what's right.

The truth cuts deep.

Some people
only want you
the moment they feel

you don't belong to them
at all.

FEEL SOMETHING

I need you to feel something.

To take whatever it is
you have
and make something beautiful
out of it.

To take the moment
no matter how tragic

you think it is
and appreciate it
for what it is.

I need you to stop
kicking yourself around.

To stop thinking
your life is shit,

and to stop doubting
everything and everyone
you come across.

My god,
not everyone is out
to get you.
Not everything is meant

to bring you harm.

Where's your goddamn heart?
Your goddamn courage?

I know you don't expect
yourself to be this strong,

to be this tolerant
but I am telling you,

you got one hell of a fight
in you.

I've seen it
and I know you've seen it
too.

So why give up this easily?
Why shut yourself
from the feeling, the possibility?

You have this profound
fire in you.

So why not let it out,
why not set it free?

Why not face
the devouring past
and stand up to it?

You have so much to offer
and you should never dwell
on what aches.

That kind of worry
doesn't look good on you

but of course,
that's easier said than done,
right?

And who the hell
am I
to tell you what's right,
right?

You have to live
for what you believe in
and be careful who
you trust.

And know
that out of pain
comes the most beautiful
of things.

It's the universe's way
of telling you,

you're capable
of so much more.

THE LITTLE 9MM

I feel so fragile at times.

Like I'm about to break
over anything,
explode, snap, you know?

The rage rivers
through the blood

and the burning of trees
sway in and out
of the lungs.

Anything switches me on.

From noise
to light
to crowds
and lies.

It ticks,
rubs me the wrong way.

The traffic.
The tardiness.
The orders.

The books.

The poetry.
The readers.
The fans.

The mind.
The pain.
The sweat
and the insomnia.

It all,
at times devours me whole.

I feel like I can't
take it anymore.

Like the shield
is calling my name.

Whispering,
telling me to hold it
in the palm of my hands.

Comforting me,
flirting and persuading me
to keep its steel skin warm.

That's all it says to me.

It tells me not
to calm down.

To use this rage
and pull myself off the edge.

Off this plane.
Off this lonely dimension.

If I am sick
then perhaps,
the shield is too.

Perhaps,
we share this common bond,
this sacred brotherhood.

So we made a pact,
one we must keep

till the darkness swells
throughout the room.

And it is
to visit it the next time
my heart is boiling.

The next time
I feel as if I can no longer
go on.

The shield gives me life,
and it promised to always be there—
waiting—as long as I visit it

from time to time.

No one wants to feel alone.
Everyone deserves
a little company,

even if we know
it is only

for a little while.

I FEEL EMPTY SOMETIMES

I put my heart into this.
I put my soul
and because of it
sometimes I feel empty.

But nonetheless,
it is all for a good cause.

It is all for the empowerment
of other people.

The healing
of other people
and myself.

I take my pain,
extract it from the depths
of my wounds
and from it
grows something beautiful.

Like a flower.
A moon.
A star.

A goddamn ocean.

And they are

the size of two
supernovas
swallowing my pride whole.

I am vulnerable.
I am cold.
I am alone.
I am absent.
I am no longer here.

But it is all
for a cause.

To leave my heart open,
up for grabs
like treasure washing up
the shore.

If I am sad
it is only to give you laughter.

If I am lost
it is only to guide you home.

What I make,
this art,
this isolation from the world
is only to give you
comfort and peace.

My pain

is your glory
and out of my ashes
you will build anew person.

And you will understand
yourself more
than I could have ever

understood myself
to begin with.

So take it.
It is yours.

My soul will show you the way.

And the traffic lights continue.
And the people keep passing by.

And the playgrounds stay empty…

but none of it really matters
unless you care…

yourself.

THE LONG TRAVEL

Your edges are not fragile.

So give yourself
a little credit for how far
you've come.

For how strong you've grown.

It's not everyday
that you realize this,

but you should always
admire yourself

for who you've become.

THE FIRST DAY OF THE YEAR

He smoked fourteen grams
of marijuana on New Year's Eve.

Alone and unwanted.
Starved of affection and love.

Outside,
sitting on the floor with no one,
nothing but the intensity

to run away from it all.

Without having the luxury to escape
all things that hurt and bring pain.

2017 has been good,
too good
but not fulfilling enough.

Five tokes in.
There is no change
in what shakes the soul.

No movement.

Nothing noticeable
to raise the dead.
The fireworks bang.

Like gunshots
in the middle of water.

He inhales the gun powder
that stretches through the air.

Bang.
Bang.
Bang.

Goes the mind.
Goes the sweet human heart.

And the soul begins to tick.
It begins to look
and make sense of all
that has been lost and forgotten.

The time is his.

The tragic taste
of loneliness.

It hits him
like a wild train.

Off rail and boundless
of its course.

The heart begins to flutter.
The scent of death

and confusion walk hand in hand.

They greet him.
Alongside they smile
and walk him inside the house.

He loses feeling.

He loses his words
and reasonable senses
to the smoke of the land.

To the burning pleasures
the Earth brings.

He searches for god,
but god does not reveal himself.

The prayers of life
go unanswered.

He thinks he's going to die.

Thought after thought.

The loss of control
and the panic enters the room.

The heart continues to beat.
Faster and faster.
So fast

he no longer believes
it is pumping.

The slow exhale.
The slow passing of time.

This is the end.
The last minute of the show,
the grand spectacle.

He is doomed.
We are all doomed.

And the smoke,
the breath of life
is returned back
to where it came from.

The gods laugh at him.

Point
and joke about the errors
he makes.

Fourteen grams.

That is all it takes
to see him.

To feel like the touch of death
is caressing the skin.

Slowly it fades away.
It goes into nothing.
It goes within.

An hour later he speaks.
He feels as if he's been released.

As if he's finally taking
his first breath of life.

His heart rate
goes back to normal.

And the paranoia steps off
with a warm farewell.

The trip is worth it
he says.

It gives him perspective
on what matters.

On what really warms
the human soul.

Friends.
Family.
Connectivity to those
around you.
The knowledge of oneself

and the recognition
of one's true feelings.

That is where it is at.
That is where perfect nirvana
is born.

He laughs at almost dying,
at feelings as if
it is his last night on earth…

as he welcomes the new year
a new man.

Fourteen grams is all it took.

Fourteen grams may kill you
or make you feel as if
you're going to die,

but also fourteen grams
can make you realize

there's so much more
than this.

SHE WAS...

She was,
if anything,
more than just a woman.

She was someone
who would get down
to it, that is,

what you were feeling.

She understood people,
she knew
how to break them down...

how to drift them apart
to bring them back together again.

And it was terrifying
how accurate she was.

If she said something,
it was probably right.

Therefore,
everyone listened.

She was more,
so much more.

This,
I tell you,

women stop becoming women
the moment you give them
a chance.

When you give them
the opportunity,
they become saviors,

they become listeners,
healers, beacons
to those who feel lost.

They become
these brave beautiful creatures
full of wisdom

and wit,
and most of the time
they'll change your life
for the best—quicker

than you can
blink your eyes.

IT CAN BE

What a beautiful thing
it can be—to follow your heart

without getting it broken.

To feel love
without getting hurt.

And to take the things
you said
back—without completely

destroying someone
you once cared about.

THE AGE COMES IN

I think the older you get
the harder it is
to let go of someone.

The harder it is
to say good-bye.

I think,
yes,
with age comes wisdom
but also

comes the realization
of what's important.

And when you lose someone,
it feels like the end
of the world

but as an adult,
you know,
you have to learn
how to suck it up.

How to deal with it.

How to pretend
everything is okay,

although
it's not.

That's what growing up is like.
What responsibility
is like

and it's harsh.

It's sad.
It's hard.

Life isn't easy
and loving someone
doesn't make it any easier.

Because

love is hard.
Making it work is hard,

and letting go
is even harder.

People will always
be people

but the moment
you love someone,

they become

so much more.

And every day
someone loses someone.

And every night
someone decides *not* to stay.

While letting go
becomes a part of our lives

and saying good-bye
feels a little too familiar

year after year...

as everyone you love
begins to disappear.

NEVER WERE

I'm letting you go
and maybe I need this
more than you.

Maybe I need
to spend time on myself.

To breathe.
To grow
and to wrap my arms
around my heart
and whisper:

"You're not alone.
You never will be
and never were."

WHAT I SAY

As time goes on,
I have to remind myself
how I don't need
people to agree
with me.

How I don't need them
to understand
and make sense of all the
messes I've left behind.

What I need is…

I need them to stop telling me
how to live my life.

To stop hating the parts of me
they can't relate to.

If someone wants to
be my friend,
I need them
to drop the labels.

To drop everything they've learned
about relationships

and just let things be.

Let things move naturally.

Imagine that,
meeting someone
and not having to worry

about being judged
or meeting someone,

and not having to pretend
to be someone else—

in order to be loved
at all.

HEAL AND GROW

Everything you are
and everything you will ever be

is because

someone took the time
to love you.

The time to listen to you,
and mold you
into who you are.

Give back.

Someone out there
needs your time.

Your experience.

Give back.

Someone out there
is waiting for you
to help them with their
life.

Positivity is
a beautiful thing

and there's nothing better

than watching someone
you care about

heal and grow.

LITTLE EXPLOSIONS

The best of you is gone.

And now,
against the grain,

against time
and all things that do
not matter.

I sit here
on an old squeaking chair
behind an old tumbling desk.

Drinking.
Thinking.

Missing the past
for what it was,
what it is
and what it means
to me.

With gentle music
pumping through the radio.

Back and forth
and then back again.

I reminisce of the way
your hair would sway.

The way your scent
devoured the room

like healthy veins
on the wall.

The best of you is gone,
the best of me...is gone.

I repeat to myself.

It has all gone through
the closed window.

And now what remains
are these small little
explosions,

these ticking time bombs
that go off silently

that go off
the same way
love goes off

or on.

I rock the chair some more.

Drink some more.
Think some more.

Hurt even more.

The pain swells.
It stings.

The wound has never healed.

I miss you
for everything you
once gave me

and for everything
I never received.

And my hands are now
left alone,

reaching out,
looking for their other half

but nothing reaches back.

And the chair
keeps rocking.

And the mail
keeps coming in.

And my heart
keeps changing…

and all the best
parts of you

are still gone.

AVOID AT ALL COST

You are not public property.

Not everyone should be allowed
to disappoint you.

Not everyone should be allowed
to walk away.

Because there are just some things
I know you don't deserve,

and having people
play with your heart
is one of them.

It should be
on top of your list

of things to avoid.

THE SWEET TRUTH

Yes,
it is true,

I want to be more
than just friends.

I want to be lovers.

I want to be
that person you wake up
thinking of
and call in the middle
of the night.

It is true,
you make me feel good,
very good
as if nothing matters.

You make me think
of all my sorrows,

of all my
beautiful memories
all at once.

That's a rare thing.
To make me feel

as if
I'm in the past
holding on
to the future.

It's bright.

Sometimes hot
and too fragile to hold.

It aches.

That's how much
this means to me.

It wakes me
and doesn't let me rest.

It is true,
if I must put it into words
then all I have said

means nothing

because I have no vocabulary
to express
what you make me feel.

If it is
too much
or too little,

it doesn't matter.

What does is
that I want to be more
than just friends.

With no apologies
and no regrets.

You give me purpose—
a life worth living.

A time so delicate
it can't be wasted.

So this I tell to you.

I want to be more
than just friends,
sweet darling,

and that is
the only truth
I know.

LISTEN TO YOURSELF

It's about who you want.

Who you think of the most.

It's about who's on your mind
when you're awake
and who crosses it

when you're about
to slumber.

That's who your heart
belongs to—that's the only person

that matters.

The one who keeps you company
when you feel most alone.

That's who you love.

Your story begins
and ends with that person.

THE OCEANS ARE...

The oceans are heavy.
The sky is heavy.

The mountains
and the land are heavy.

The sadness piles over
and the tears roll down

the rivers and streets.

We are sad.
We are broken.

We are looking for ways
to get out.

Our hearts are heavy.
Our thoughts are heavy.

Our feelings and past,

too heavy.

Our bodies have become
houses of pain.

Buildings and temples

of suffering.
It is okay…
to cry.

To lose sleep.
To trust no one.

The dreams are heavy.

The depths of one's eyes
are heavy.

And the hues of broken love
are heavy.

We don't know
who we are anymore.

We have lost believing.

The end is near
and it is heavy.

And the crowds can't move.
And the planes

and ships can't fly or sail.

And the people want peace.
And the politicians want war.

And the countries want
a little more…

but it is all
still

too heavy…

to claim
as your own.

EXPECT NOTHING

It works both ways.

You cannot expect
to receive
and never give.

You cannot expect
to succeed without failing—

to love
without getting hurt.

Life is hard,
yet,
it is perfectly balanced.

Sometimes
you are going to get burned,

while other times,
you will unwillingly scorch

those around you.

That is how it works.

You win some,
you lose some

and in the long run,
everyone gets

a lesson
or a blessing

in return.

I THINK I KNOW

I know by experience
that what you're feeling

right now

will not last forever.

Nothing is permanent,
and if you want to live
life to the fullest,

you must live
in the moment
every chance you can.

That is how
you will find meaning:

in everything
you have to gain
and lose.

In everything
you will learn
and not have the opportunity
to know.

In all the people

you will love
and all the strangers
you will dream of—

but never have the chance
to meet.

Life's greatest loss is

believing all that you hold
is yours to keep...

forever.

Appreciate everything
for what it is.

From friendships
to feelings to moments.

Hold on to them
while you can.

Love them dearly,
and don't forget

to *always* remember that.

NO WORDS NEEDED

But it's true,
you can fall in love

with people's souls.

With people's gestures,
hearts and morals.

With people's smiles
and with people's minds—

without exchanging

a single kiss,

and without saying
a single word.

PERSONAL

Everyone is going through
their own personal dilemma.

So please be kind.

Speak gently
and give people chances.

You never know
whose life

you're changing.

WOUNDS ARE HEAVY

These wounds I carry
cannot be concealed.

Therefore,
if you wish to sit
beside me,

if you wish to love me,
and break me down—
make sense of the darkness
within me,

then you must understand
how most people
have failed to love me.

How most
have tried to figure me out
and can't understand
where it all went wrong.

But the truth is,
not many would know
what to do with love

if it came knocking
at their front door,
and not many

would recognize it
if it passed right by them.

It's sad,
when I think of it.

In order to love me,
you must first know my flaws,
what angers me—
what drives me off the wall.

You must know everything,
or at least die trying.

And I'm pretty sure
that's how it goes

for everyone
around the world.

You have to love all
of me...

or not love me at all.